PET
Practice Tests 1

*Diana L. Fried-Booth and
Louise Hashemi*

CAMBRIDGE
UNIVERSITY PRESS

Published by the Press Syndicate of the University of Cambridge
The Pitt Building, Trumpington Street, Cambridge CB2 1RP
40 West 20th Street, New York, NY 10011–4211, USA
10 Stamford Road, Oakleigh, Melbourne 3166, Australia

© Cambridge University Press 1988

First published 1988
Sixth printing 1993

Printed in Great Britain
by Scotprint Ltd, Musselburgh

ISBN 0 521 33819 0 Student's Book
ISBN 0 521 33820 4 Teacher's Book
ISBN 0 521 32883 7 Set of 2 cassettes

Contents

Thanks

We should like to thank all the students and staff at the various schools where the material for *PET Practice Tests 1* was piloted who took the time and trouble to record their comments and reactions. Particular thanks also to the students and staff at The Chichester School of English who contributed towards producing 'sample' answers for the final version of the Teacher's Book. We are also indebted to Jeanne McCarten and Margherita Baker at Cambridge University Press for all their encouragement and support during the writing and revision of this material.

Acknowledgements

The authors and publishers are grateful to Trust House Forte for permission to reproduce their text on pp. 42–3.

Photographs by Abbas and Louise Hashemi on pp. 1, 2, 19, 20, 37, 38, 55, 56, 73 and 74; Jeremy Pembrey on pp. 16, 32, 33, 51, 68, 69, 85 and 86.
Drawings by Clyde Pearson on pp. 5, 32, 35, 49, 67, 84, 85 and 87; Chris Evans on pp. 14, 15, 27, 47, 49, 50, 51 and 85; Leslie Marshall on pp. 18, 22, 31, 32, 58, 67, 68 and 69.
Artwork by Peter Ducker and Wenham Arts.

Colour Oral Section: TV programme details (4A) by permission of *The Independent* newspaper; photographs by Jeremy Pembrey (1B, 1C, 5A, 5B), Abbas Hashemi (2B) and Barnaby's Picture Library (3C, 3D); artwork by Ace Art.

Book design by Peter Ducker MSTD.

Introduction to the student

This book is for students who are preparing to take the Preliminary English Test (PET). It contains five units or practice tests. The first four are based on different topics: hotels, restaurants and accommodation; entertainment; sport and leisure; the media. These units will help you to learn and revise the vocabulary and structures which are covered in your coursebook. The last unit, which is like the 'real' PET, is *not* based on a particular topic. This unit can be used as a final practice test just before you take the examination.

If you work through this book it will help you to recognise the kinds of questions you will have to answer in the examination. There are four parts in each test: reading, writing, listening and speaking, although the oral section of the test is taken separately.

The book is meant to be used in class with a teacher but you can use it if you are working alone to practise the reading, writing and listening parts of the test.

If you are studying by yourself you will need the cassettes, which contain the recordings for the listening part of the test, and the Teacher's Book, which contains the answer Key for all the exercises and the tapescripts of the recordings. You will probably need extra help with the speaking part of the test, so ask a teacher or a native speaker to help you.

We hope that you will enjoy using the book (even if you don't finally take the examination). Good Luck!

Unit 1   Hotels, restaurants and accommodation

READING

QUESTION 1

Look at the five pictures of signs below. Someone asks you what each sign means. For each sign put a cross in one of the boxes – like this X – to show the correct answer.

1.

☐ Go this way.

☐ Don't close the door.

☐ Don't go inside.

☐ Knock and enter.

2.

☐ Don't lock the room.

☐ Keep your key safe.

☐ Lock your desk before leaving.

☐ Leave your key at reception.

⟫⟫→

3.

☐ You can only have a meal if you have booked.

☐ You do not need to reserve a table.

☐ The restaurant is not open this evening.

☐ If you wait you will be given a table.

4.

☐ You must carry your luggage yourself.

☐ Porters are available if necessary.

☐ A porter will come if you ring.

☐ Ask a porter if you need your luggage.

5.

☐ You cannot bring your luggage into the dining room.

☐ You must look after your things yourself.

☐ You should give your things to the manager.

☐ You should lock things in your suitcase.

QUESTION 2

Read the article below and circle the letter next to the word that best fits each space.

EXAMPLE: I can strongly .... this restaurant.

      A tell   B try   Ⓒ recommend   D offer

A new restaurant with a difference has opened in the High Street next door to the Royal Theatre in Bristol. It is called 'Starters' and is (1)............... by Carol and Philip Wells who opened a (2)............... restaurant in London last year.

Instead of a traditional three-course (3)..............., customers can choose whatever (4)............... want from a list of (5)............... a hundred starters or first courses. The list also includes recipes from all over the world and customers are recommended to (6)............... at least 3 starters to (7)............... a satisfying meal.

Prices vary depending on what you have, (8)............... it is possible to eat quite cheaply if you (9)............... want to spend a lot of money. The new restaurant is becoming very popular and it's (10)............... to book a table to avoid waiting.

1.   A got   B held   C run   D taken

2.   A similar   B same   C several   D like

3.   A tea   B meal   C food   D plate

4.   A you   B he   C they   D we

5.   A only   B up   C more   D over

6.   A read   B choose   C look   D want

7.   A make   B be   C want   D need

8.   A so   B then   C unless   D if

9.   A do   B can   C don't   D will

10. A well   B best   C great   D fine

QUESTION 3

Look at the advertisement below for the restaurants and then answer the questions.

A

The Coffee Shop

Relax in our comfortable chairs and enjoy our excellent fresh coffee, tea and hot chocolate or cooling fruit juices – choose from all sorts of cakes, bread and biscuits baked in our own kitchen. Cooked breakfasts to order until 10a.m.

Open 06.30 – 18.30

E

'Round the World' Dining Room

Leave the grey skies of England behind you for a couple of hours when you step in to try our large range of food from all over the world. Our waiters are only too happy to explain our menu so if you want to try something new, come and see us.

Open Noon – Midnight

B

Serve Yourself

Eat as much as you can for only £5!! Choose from dozens of delicious soups, salads, cold meats and cheeses. For the younger members of the family we offer reduced prices along with free colouring books and pencils.

Open Noon – 3 and 5 – 10

Eating out at
FIVE WAYS
◆
The choice is yours!

THE SANDWICH BAR

Your choice of over 50 different fillings for a sandwich made to order!! To drink, choose from delicious hot coffee, a wide selection of top soft drinks or ice cold milk. Our quick service makes this the best place for busy shoppers or anyone short of time!

Open 9a.m. – 2p.m.

The Steak House

Friendly candle-lit restaurant serving traditional British steak suppers as well as French and Italian meals. Choose your own steak for our chef to cook to your personal taste. £15 includes a large selection of fresh vegetables, a sweet course and a drink with your meal.

Open 7.30p.m. 'til Midnight

D

C

The five groups of people below are hoping to eat at one of the restaurants. Read what each of them says and write the letter A, B, C, D or E in the box next to them to show which restaurant you think they will go to.

Time	People	What they want	Which restaurant?

1. **10:00** — 'I had to get up early this morning. I'd like to sit and have a cup of tea and a biscuit somewhere quiet and pleasant before I start my shopping.' ☐

2. **12:30** — 'It's my lunch hour and I'm in a hurry – a glass of milk and a sandwich would be ideal.' ☐

3. **13:30** — 'One of the best things about being on holiday is that you don't have to rush your meals.'

   'And we can take the opportunity to try something new – perhaps a foreign dish?' ☐

4. **17:50** — 'We're so tired! We've been shopping all day and we're all hungry.'

   'Mind you, the children don't eat much – they always start playing around before we've finished.' ☐

5. **21:00** — 'It's my birthday – I'd really like something special – what about something from abroad?'

   'That'd be fun for you but I'd rather not eat foreign food myself.' ☐

5

QUESTION 4

Lakeshire Tourist Board keeps a list of holiday accommodation in order to be able to advise tourists looking for somewhere to stay in the area.
Here are five of the places they may recommend. Look at the information below and then put a cross in the box for numbers 1–10 if a statement is correct.

LAKESHIRE TOURIST BOARD

Holiday Accommodation List   ref: CL/AF   file: 3A

Address: Bullock House,
Great Pannington

Tel. no: 61355
Owner: Mr and Mrs Stouts *(v. friendly)*
Owner's address if non-resident: ———

Tel. no: ———
Description: Old stone farmhouse. Beautiful views of surrounding hills.

Accommodation available:
3 bedrooms. All have own shower & TV. Children's beds available. Small sitting-room for guests' use.
Services:
Breakfasts; evening meals. *(Good home cooking).*

Notes: Family home of Stouts for many generations. Opened for guests this year. No dogs. No central heating! Limited parking space — car owners should check when booking.

LAKESHIRE TOURIST BOARD

Holiday Accommodation List   ref: CL/AF   file: 2A

Address: Mills Cottage, End Green, Near Pendle.

Tel. no: ———
Owner: J. Bright
Owner's address if non-resident:
Uppercross, Pendle.

Tel. no: 61396
Description: Former farm cottage. Near busy little market town.

To rent weekly from May → September

Accommodation available:
Kitchen, living-room, 2 × double bedrooms. Bathroom (not very modern!)
Services:
T.V in sitting-room No heating in bedrooms. Large garden with plenty of parking space.

Notes: No animals in cottage.
NB   Guests provide own sheets and towels

LAKESHIRE TOURIST BOARD

Holiday Accommodation List ref: JB/ML file: 3A

Address: GRACE FARM, PENDLE

Tel. no: 61321
Owner: MR & MRS FREELING
Owner's address if non-resident: —

Tel. no: —
Description: 16th century farmhouse

Accommodation available: 2 double bedrooms with private showers. Central heating throughout.

Services: Meals: breakfast only. Sandwiches made to order for picnics.
* Horses can be hired. Fishing in river behind house.
Notes: No dogs.
* Mrs Freeling will give riding lessons when not too busy.

LAKESHIRE TOURIST BOARD

Holiday Accommodation List ref: JB/CL file: 3A

Address: Hollow Castle, Pendlebury

Tel. no: —
Owner: Mr and Mrs Agremont
Owner's address if non-resident: —

Tel. no: 60227
Description: Family home in eighteenth century castle.

Accommodation available:
Several comfortable guest rooms.

Services:
All meals. [Excellent cooking!!]

Notes: Attractive garden with parking space.
Open all year round. No phone. No dogs

LAKESHIRE TOURIST BOARD

Holiday Accommodation List   ref: JB/AF   file: 1B
_____

Address: Elmslie Grove, Lake Drive, Pendlebury

Tel. no: 61296
Owner: Mrs V. Bright
Owner's address if non-resident: ―

Tel. no: ―
Description: Old country house (Beautiful building overlooking Blue Lake)

Accommodation available: 6 double bedrooms. 2 single. (Some with private bathrooms)

Services: Traditional breakfasts and dinners. Children's early suppers available.

Notes: Only a few minutes from Sailing Club. Popular with fishermen and walkers. Many guests return regularly every year. [Early booking essential] Well-behaved dogs accepted.

1. All these places have telephones. ☐

2. There is a large garage for guests' cars at Bullock House. ☐

3. Mills Cottage is suitable for four people. ☐

4. Elmslie Grove was opened to guests last year. ☐

5. Bullock House is suitable for families. ☐

6. Mills Cottage is a long way from any shops. ☐

7. You can see the Blue Lake from Elmslie Grove. ☐

8. Hollow Castle is older than Grace Farm. ☐

9. Mrs Freeling sometimes gives riding lessons to guests. ☐

10. The Agremonts provide lunch if you want it. ☐

QUESTION 5

Read this passage and then answer the questions below. You must put a cross in the correct box or write in a few words.

I must tell you about our holiday this year – it was one of the best we'd ever had. No, we weren't staying in an expensive hotel, but a youth hostel! I know what you're thinking: we must've gone mad. But we haven't – I just wish we'd discovered youth hostels years ago. Now that I'm back at university again luxury hotels are a thing of the past, and I was complaining about this one day to a friend who said that she and her family never stayed anywhere but hostels. I had no idea that hostels could be anything from a cottage to a castle. I mean where else do you get to stay in a castle! In fact there are four different grades – simple, standard, superior and special so you pay an overnight charge according to the kind of hostel you stay at. You can't stay more than three nights at a time but that didn't bother us because we wanted a touring holiday. Basically you look after yourself although most hostels do breakfast and some of them offer an evening meal if you arrive early enough. There are a few rules like having to be in by 11 p.m. in the evening and out by 10 a.m. in the morning but otherwise you're free to do what you want. Now I really believe that the best thing about this whole holiday was meeting so many different and interesting people. I used to think hostels were only for the young and noisy, but not any more. You can't imagine what a variety there was! Anyway, what arc you all doing next year?

1. This text is from ☐ a diary.

    ☐ a letter.

    ☐ a magazine.

    ☐ a poster.

2. What is the writer trying to do? ☐ to give directions

    ☐ to offer instructions

    ☐ to make complaints

    ☐ to give information

3. Why didn't the writer stay in a hotel?

    ....

    ....

⋙→

4. What did the writer most enjoy about her holiday?

    ....

    ....

5. Only one of these people will choose to stay in a Youth Hostel. Show which one you think it will be by circling the letter A, B, C or D.

    A   I cook for my family all the year round, and although I enjoy doing it, I really don't want to have to provide any meals when I'm on holiday especially as I plan to go out and enjoy myself, dancing the night away!

    B   I've worked hard for many years and now I've got a bit of free time I aim to see as many different places as possible. If I can save on the cost of accommodation, I'll have more to spend on train or bus fares.

    C   We want an opportunity to meet different sorts of people and get to know them so thought we'd spend a couple of weeks relaxing in one place – our jobs mean moving about so much that it would be nice not to carry a suitcase for a fortnight!

    D   I'm a student and I don't have a lot of money to spare. I don't like getting cold and wet though, so if the weather isn't good I'll just make myself a pot of coffee and stay in all day reading an exciting book.

WRITING

QUESTION 6

Here are some sentences about a café called Checkers. Finish the second sentence so that it has the same meaning as the first.

EXAMPLE: The café belongs to Jane.

It's Jane's café.

1. Checkers was opened in 1984 by Jane Williams.

    Jane Williams..

2. The café has a lot of tables.

    There...

3. You'll avoid waiting by booking a table in advance.

    If..

4. You have to pay about £10 for a three-course meal.

    A three-course meal...

5. The café is considered to be very good.

    Everyone..

QUESTION 7

An English friend has asked you to recommend a couple of hotels in your town/city where he or she could stay for a few nights. Write the details in the spaces provided.

Name of hotel:....................................

Address: ....

....

Number of rooms:...............................

Price: ....

....

Bedrooms: ....

....

....

....

Food: ....

....

....

Extra things provided

by the hotel: ....

....

....

....

General comments:.............................

....

....

....

Name of hotel:....................................

Address: ....

....

Number of rooms:...............................

Price: ....

....

Bedrooms: ....

....

....

....

Food: ....

....

....

Extra things provided

by the hotel: ....

....

....

....

General comments:.............................

....

....

....

QUESTION 8

You have just spent a week at the Milford Hotel. Before you leave you fill in the form below by ticking the boxes 1–4. Now complete the rest of the form by writing in the details and suggestions. Write about 75 words.

MILFORD HOTEL

1. Your room   ☺ ☐   😐 ☑   ☹ ☐   3. The service   ☺ ☐   😐 ☐   ☹ ☑

2. The food   ☺ ☐   😐 ☐   ☹ ☑   4. Your stay   ☺ ☐   😐 ☐   ☹ ☑

Please give details about the things that you have found unsatisfactory. Do you have any suggestions or comments which would help us to make your next stay more comfortable?

. . . .

. . . .

. . . .

. . . .

. . . .

. . . .

. . . .

. . . .

. . . .

. . . .

. . . .

. . . .

. . . .

. . . .

. . . .

. . . .

. . . .

. . . .

LISTENING

QUESTION 9

Put a cross in the box you think is the most suitable.

EXAMPLE:

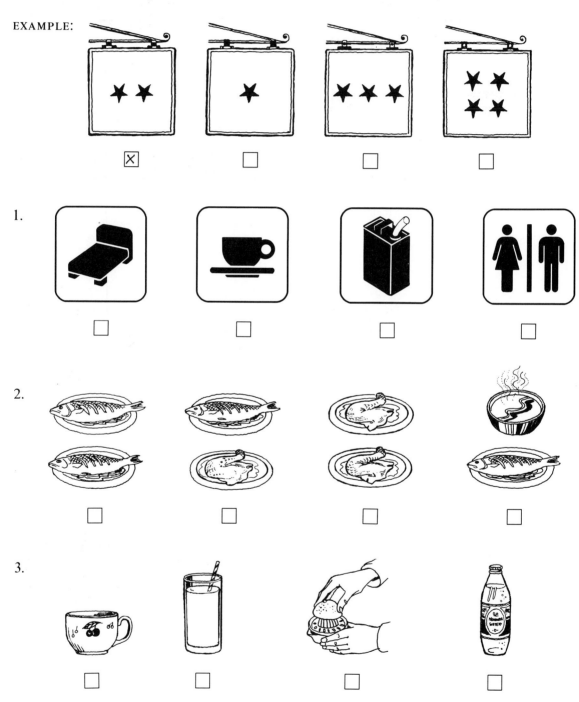

4.

☐   ☐

☐   ☐

5.

☐   ☐   ☐   ☐

6.

☐   ☐   ☐   ☐

》》》→

7.

☐

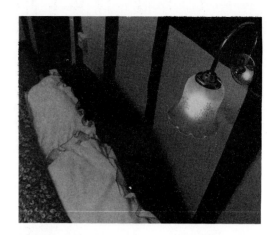
☐

☐

☐

QUESTION 10

Listen to Wendy talking to a group of people and put a cross in the boxes you think are the most suitable.

1. The dining-room opens for breakfast from 7.00 to 7.30. ☐
7.00 to 8.30. ☐
7.30 to 8.30. ☐
8.30 to 9.30. ☐

2. The packed lunches can be collected from Wendy. ☐

    the porter. ☐

    the dining-room. ☐

    the kitchen staff. ☐

3. This group will have dinner in the restaurant. ☐

    in the garden room. ☐

    on the beach. ☐

    in their rooms. ☐

4. On Tuesday night the holiday makers can go to a film festival. ☐

    flower festival. ☐

    food festival. ☐

    dance festival. ☐

5. On Wednesday evening there will be a beach party. ☐

    fishing trip. ☐

    moonlight walk. ☐

    swimming party. ☐

6. Wendy is a waitress. ☐

    holiday maker. ☐

    doctor. ☐

    holiday guide. ☐

QUESTION 11

Write in the information needed below.

(1) ___ _____ *Street Bistro*

Open from 12 – (2) _____

Price (3) _____

includes
    soup
    main course
    fruit or (4) _____

Tel: (5) _____

(6) _____ *Restaurant*

Open from (7) _____- *2 am*

Speciality (8) _____
          always fresh

Price (9) _____

Tel: (10) _____

QUESTION 12

If you agree with the statement put a cross in the box under 'Yes'. If you do not agree, cross the box under 'No'.

		Yes	No
1.	The wife has discussed holiday accommodation at her office.	☐	☐
2.	The husband likes camping.	☐	☐
3.	The wife is willing to do some housework when she's on holiday.	☐	☐
4.	The husband is more worried about saving money than the wife.	☐	☐
5.	The couple will probably choose bed and breakfast accommodation.	☐	☐

Unit 2 Entertainment

READING

QUESTION 1

Look at the five pictures of signs below. Someone asks you what each sign means. For each sign put a cross in one of the boxes – like this X – to show the correct answer.

1.

   ☐ Tickets can be returned here.

   ☐ Tickets are available outside.

   ☐ All the tickets have been sold.

   ☐ There are no tickets on sale yet.

2.

   ☐ There is no more room.

   ☐ There are no more seats.

   ☐ There is room for one more person.

   ☐ There is only one more room.

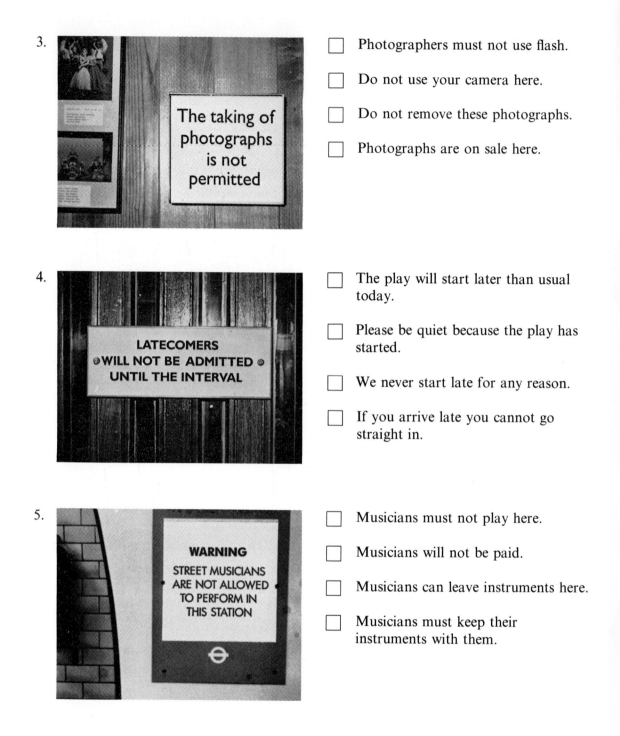

3.
- [ ] Photographers must not use flash.
- [ ] Do not use your camera here.
- [ ] Do not remove these photographs.
- [ ] Photographs are on sale here.

The taking of photographs is not permitted

4.
- [ ] The play will start later than usual today.
- [ ] Please be quiet because the play has started.
- [ ] We never start late for any reason.
- [ ] If you arrive late you cannot go straight in.

LATECOMERS WILL NOT BE ADMITTED UNTIL THE INTERVAL

5.
- [ ] Musicians must not play here.
- [ ] Musicians will not be paid.
- [ ] Musicians can leave instruments here.
- [ ] Musicians must keep their instruments with them.

WARNING
STREET MUSICIANS ARE NOT ALLOWED TO PERFORM IN THIS STATION

QUESTION 2

Read the article below and circle the letter next to the word that best fits each space.

EXAMPLE: The .... between the acts was twenty minutes long.

       A   time   Ⓑ interval   C space   D pause

'The Moon Trap' is a new film made by a young Canadian (1)............... called Melvin Strang. The main parts in the film are (2)............... by Sid Cheung and Julie Plein who last appeared in 'Music For Ever'.

In this new film (3)............... star as a young married couple who buy an old house in the country. After living there (4)............... a few weeks strange things begin to happen.

Some of the furniture in the house disappears and can't be (5)...............; windows break and pictures fall off walls. At night they (6)............... crying noises, and when the moon is up loud screams can be heard from the woods nearby.

As you might expect, the young couple try to discover the (7)............... for all these strange events and this leads them into some very frightening situations. (8)............... you are easily scared don't go and see this film! But if you enjoy films with (9)............... of adventure and murder (10)............... this is the film for you.

1. A actor   B leader   C director   D manager

2. A played   B given   C made   D put

3. A the   B they   C she   D them

4. A since   B from   C for   D by

5. A taken   B moved   C made   D found

6. A hear   B make   C seem   D sound

7. A way   B course   C reason   D use

8. A Why   B If   C How   D Because

9. A lots   B much   C many   D all

10. A as   B when   C than   D then

QUESTION 3

Read this information about an international festival and then answer the questions.

FESTIVAL 22nd May – 9th June

ART

Displays of paintings, drawings and photographs from Europe and Asia are all part of the Festival programme, with a total of more than 400 pieces of work to be seen.

Early 20th century advertisements will be on display at this year's Festival. Copies of the above advertisement are on sale at the Box Office.

MUSIC

There will be a huge range of music in this year's Festival from 14th century dance music to modern jazz. Many famous musicians will be visiting the Festival as well as at least two internationally famous orchestras.

Lunchtime concerts – Every day of the Festival!

All lunchtime concerts begin at 1.00 p.m. and last approximately 55 minutes. Except on Monday 26th May* they are in the Guildhall; all tickets are priced £2.00.

* in the Church Hall.

HOW TO BOOK

Telephone reservations: 63362/66411 from 1st April.
    Payment for tickets reserved by telephone must be received at the Festival Box Office within 3 days. The tickets will then be sent by post.
    Personal booking: From 1st May the Festival Box Office will be open as follows:
Monday to Saturday 9.30 a.m. – 5.30 p.m.
Sunday (during the Festival only) 9.30 a.m. – 1.00 p.m.

Look at the information and then put a cross in the box for numbers 1–10 if a statement is correct.

1.   The Festival begins in May.   ☐

2.   The Festival includes many kinds of music.   ☐

3.   You can see more than 400 drawings in the art show.   ☐

4.   The lunchtime concerts are more than an hour long.   ☐

5.   You can buy copies of the early 20th century advertisements.   ☐

6.   Tickets for the concerts cost between £3.00 and £6.00.   ☐

7.   All the concerts are in the Guildhall.   ☐

8.   You can book by phone from April 1st.   ☐

9.   The box office is open every day in May.   ☐

10.   You can apply for tickets in person in April.   ☐

QUESTION 4

Look at the information about these plays which you can see in December. Decide which play you would recommend these people to see and write the letter A, B, C, D, E or F in the box next to them to show which play you think they should go to.

ARTS & AMENITIES COMMITTEE

City Theatre Guide

DECEMBER

A

CITY HALL

Wellington Sq.

GOD'S WONDERFUL RAILWAY

by ACH Smith

Tues–Sat
7.30 nightly
£5, £8, £9.50

All seats £5
(under 14, half price)

The story of the Great Western Railway and the men involved in the building of that railway line between London and Bristol gave ACH Smith the idea for this new play. It is a mixture of songs, memories, stories and music which train lovers everywhere will enjoy.

THEATRE ROYAL

Wellington Sq.

B

JUDY

by Terry Wale

Tues–Sat
7 p.m.
Sat matinée
2.30 p.m.

A new musical play about the life of the well-known actress and singer Judy Garland. The story begins with her as a young girl and deals with both her public and private lives including her five marriages.

LITTLE THEATRE

The Greencroft

C

TWO CAN PLAY

by Trevor Rhone

Mon–Thurs
8 p.m.
£5 and £6

We are in Jamaica in the late 1970s. Now that Jim and Gloria's children have left the island to start a new life in the USA, Jim and Gloria decide to follow. This very funny play deals with the problems they have.

F

LITTLE THEATRE
continued

TYPHOID MARY

by Shirley Gee

Fri and Sat only 8 p.m. All seats £6

A true story about Mary Mallon who left Ireland at the end of the last century to work as a cook in America. Although she doesn't know it, she is carrying the terrible disease typhoid and wherever she works people fall ill. She is chased across the country by a team of doctors.

MOTHER GOOSE

by Miles Rudge

Mon–Sat 2.30 p.m. Adults £4, (under 14, £2.50)

This play is all about a goose which lays golden eggs. Originally a fairy story from France, the play is full of colour, fun, music and dance. Families with young children will find that it's ideal entertainment for a winter afternoon.

CITY ARTS CENTRE
Norfolk St

TAKING STEPS

by Alan Ayckbourn

Tues–Sat 7.30 p.m. Sat matinée 2.30 p.m. £8, £9 and £10

A very amusing play by one of Britain's most popular writers. Six people, all with their own problems, find themselves in a house which is up for sale. In one extraordinary evening they try to sort themselves out!

D

E

1. Tom and Jean:
   'We want to find something suitable for our four-year-old boys.'

2. Val and Tony:
   'We enjoy musicals and would like to learn more about famous stars.'

3. Richard:
   'I enjoy plays which make me laugh but I've already seen the one about the couple who want to go to America.'

4. Margery:
   'I saw *Judy* recently, and I'd like to see another play which uses historical facts, as long as it isn't another musical.'

5. Ruth and John:
   'We like musicals, particularly those based on historical facts, but we've also seen *Judy* already.'

QUESTION 5

Read this passage and then answer the questions below. You must put a cross in the correct box or write in a few words.

The Warren Toy Museum

This museum is in the centre of the town, a few metres from the cathedral, and near the market. It contains dolls, dolls' houses, books, games and pastimes, mechanical and constructional toys. In this collection there are toys made by all sorts of toy manufacturers from the most important to the smallest, including the most ordinary toys and the most precious. There are also records of children's pastimes over the last hundred and fifty years.

Most major manufacturing countries of Europe had toy industries in the last century; French and German factories produced millions of toys each year. Many collectors of toys think that the second half of the nineteenth century was the best period for toy production and the museum has many examples of toys from this period which are still in perfect condition. There is now a growing interest in the toys of the 1920s and 1930s and as a result of this the museum has begun to build up a collection from these years. Visitors to the museum will find that someone is always available to answer questions – we hope you will visit us.

Hours of opening 10.00–17.30
every day (except December 25 and 26)

1. This is from ☐ an advertisement.

    ☐ a school history book

    ☐ a storybook.

    ☐ a letter.

2. What is the writer trying to do? ☐ to give advice

    ☐ to give information

    ☐ to give warnings

    ☐ to give opinions

3. The museum has so many toys from the late nineteenth century because

    ....

    ....

4. Why has the museum started to collect toys from the 20th century?

....

....

5. Which of the following advertisements would you find outside the Warren Toy Museum? Put a cross in the box under the correct one.

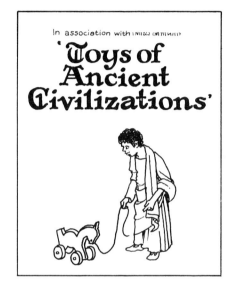

☐

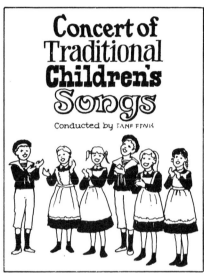

☐

☐

☐

WRITING

QUESTION 6

Here are some sentences about theatres. Finish the second sentence so that it has the same meaning as the first.

EXAMPLE: The seats near the stage are more expensive than those at the back.

The seats at the back *are cheaper than those near the stage.*

1. The National Theatre has very comfortable seats.

    The seats ....

2. Theatre seats can be booked by telephone.

    You ....

3. Theatre programmes usually have lots of information.

    There ....

4. Refreshments are sold in the intervals.

    You..

5. There is a choice of more than thirty theatres in London.

    You..

QUESTION 7

(i) *You are planning a visit to the theatre with some friends, or with your family. Look at the booking form of The Bristol Hippodrome. Choose which evening you will go, and fill in the form.*

BRISTOL HIPPODROME THEATRE

Booking information Oct 21 – Oct 26

Monday 21   CHILDREN'S MUSIC SHOW
All seats £3

Tuesday 22 to Thursday 24	SHAKESPEARE'S 'TWELFTH NIGHT' Seats £6 Half price for schoolchildren and students

Friday 25   SHAKESPEARE'S 'TWELFTH NIGHT'
All seats £7

Saturday 26 SPANISH DANCE SHOW
All seats £5
No reductions for children

ALL START AT 7 p.m.

Please fill in this form to reserve seats

Name:	Booking date:		
Address: Tel. no:			
Name of show	Date	Number of seats	Price per seat

(ii) *Now that you have booked your seats leave a* message *for your friend or family with all the details including price, time, date, where to meet, any special arrangements for transport etc. Use about 50 words.*

....

....

....

....

....

....

....

....

QUESTION 8

You have been to see one of the shows described below. Choose one and write a letter to a friend telling him or her about it. Use about 75 words.

...ector .
you in on a few th...
trade. 3 p.m. 7.30 p.m.
■ PALACE CINEMA **The Shadows** (18) 'One of the best films so far this year' The City Herald.
People die but their shadows remain! How? Why? What is the secret? Come and find out. Starring Linda Hensler and Simon Plessey.
2 p.m. 5 p.m. 8 p.m.
■ METRO **Slamdance** (15) Infidelity, jealousy and murder.
~~...~~ced thriller

...company.
■ LANTERN THEATRE **My Uncle William** Childhood memories of Uncle William. In a series of short, beautifully acted scenes, a young boy turns to a life of crime from which he cannot escape.
'One of the finest plays I've ever seen. Don't miss it.' Gwenneth Ellis, The Daily News. Booking: 262524 Tues – Sat 7.30 p.m.
■ LYRIC THEATRE ~~...~~

Meltdown party ...
Day and Bob Jones.
■ MUSIC CITY Saturday 9 p.m.
The Rockettes Live! Popular group recently returned from enormous success in Australia. Three hours of non-stop music, dance and songs. If you like good pop music book NOW!
■ THURSDAY THROWDOWN
H...

Dear . . . .,
How are you? I hope all's well with you. I'm fine and as busy as ever. I must tell you about . . . . . .

....

....

....

....

....

....

....

....

....

....

....

LISTENING

QUESTION 9

Put a cross in the box you think is the most suitable.

EXAMPLE:

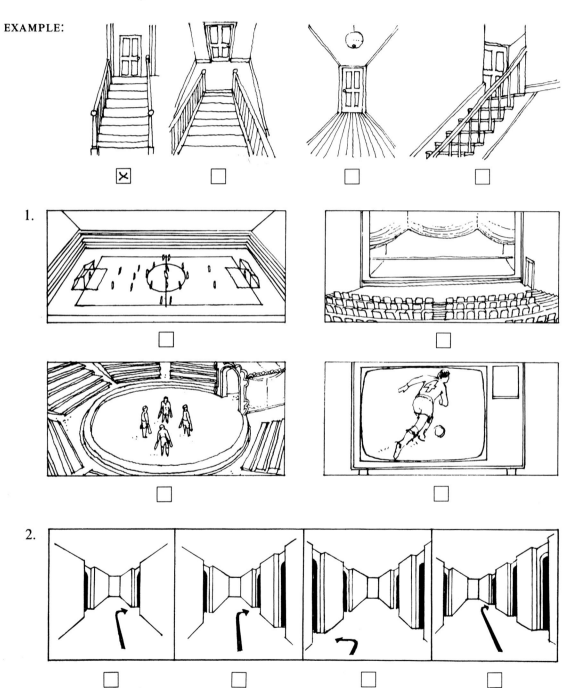

3.

☐ ☐ ☐ ☐

4.

☐

☐

☐

☐

5.

☐ ☐ ☐ ☐

6.

☐

☐

7.

QUESTION 10

In these notes put a cross in the boxes you think are the most suitable.

WHAT SHALL WE DO TODAY?

① cinema — new film on at

Odeon ☐
Regal ☐
Studio ☐
Roxy ☐

② theatre — play finishes

Saturday ☐
Tuesday ☐
Thursday ☐
Friday ☐

③ pop concert — begins

7.00 p.m. ☐
7.30 p.m. ☐
8.00 p.m. ☐
8.30 p.m. ☐

④ gallery now showing

photographs ☐
paintings ☐
drawings ☐
prints ☐

⑤ music — concert

by a river ☐
in a garden ☐
in a park ☐
in a hall ☐

⑥ museum — new collections

17th century ☐
18th century ☐
19th century ☐
20th century ☐

QUESTION 11

Write in the information needed below.

GALA CINEMA
WEEK BEGINNING OCTOBER 22

Studio One

VOYAGE TO JUPITER

Programmes at 2.30
and (1)...........................
Seat prices £3 – adults
£1.50 – children,
(2).......................... & senior citizens

Studio Two

THE MARVELLOUS

(3)...........................
Special offer this week
only – all seats
(4)...........................

Studio Three

MASTER DRAGON

One performance daily at
(5)...........................

For further information and booking

facilities 'phone (6)...........................

QUESTION 12

If you agree with the statement, put a cross in the box under 'Yes'. If you do not agree, cross the box under 'No'.

		Yes	No
1.	The boy thinks Johnny Lemons is a good singer.	☐	☐
2.	Johnny Lemons has silver hair.	☐	☐
3.	The girl thinks that Johnny Lemons' make-up is fine.	☐	☐
4.	The boy thinks that Johnny Lemons should wear stage clothes all the time.	☐	☐
5.	The girl thinks the boy's opinions are silly.	☐	☐

Unit 3 Sport and leisure

READING

QUESTION 1

Look at the five signs below. Someone asks you what each sign means. For each sign put a cross in one of the boxes – like this X – to show the correct answer.

1.

NO DOGS ALLOWED INSIDE CAMP

☐ Campers' dogs can remain here.

☐ Dogs must not be brought in here.

☐ Dogs must be looked after.

☐ A fee is charged for dogs.

2.

Shallow water NO DIVING

☐ This water is very deep.

☐ The water is not deep enough for diving.

☐ You can dive from here.

☐ The water is not deep enough for swimming.

⟫→

3.

☐ Children must not change alone.

☐ Children must use separate rooms.

☐ Parents can wait here for their children.

☐ Parents and children can change together.

4.

☐ Hand in your shoes at the sports hall.

☐ Don't leave your shoes outside the sports hall.

☐ Change your shoes before entering the sports hall.

☐ Please wear shoes all the time in the sports hall.

5.

☐ Allow plenty of time for booking.

☐ Pay when you book.

☐ Sign the book when you pay.

☐ It is too late to make a booking.

QUESTION 2

Read the article below and circle the letter next to the word that best fits each space.

EXAMPLE: She bought two tickets for the football ....

A place   Ⓑ match   C field   D play

For many young people sport is a popular part of school life and (1)............... in one of the school teams and playing in matches is v e r y i m p o r t a n t . (2)............... someone is in a team it means a lot of extra practice and often spending a Saturday or Sunday away (3)............... home, as many matches are played then.

It (4)............... also involve travelling to other towns to play against other school teams and then (5)............... on after the match for a meal or a drink.

Sometimes parents, friends or other students will travel with the team to support (6)............... own side.

When a school team wins a match it is the whole school which feels proud, (7)............... only the players. It can also mean that a school (8)............... well-known for being good at certain sports and pupils from that school may end up p l a y i n g (9)............... national and international teams so that the school has some really (10)............... names associated with it!

---

1. A having   B being   C taking   D putting

2. A If   B As   C Then   D So

3. A at   B on   C for   D from

4. A ought   B is   C can   D has

5. A being   B staying   C leaving   D spending

6. A their   B its   C our   D whose

7. A but   B however   C and   D not

8. A turns   B makes   C comes   D becomes

9. A up   B to   C for   D beside

10. A old   B new   C common   D famous

QUESTION 3

Read the descriptions below of the various activities available in Boxhampton.

Leisure in Boxhampton

This Water Park is part of the Wessex Valley Regional Park. Fishing is permitted here for Water Park Club members only (minimum age 18). Sailing, swimming and other water sports available at club, with professional teachers.

The City Farm is for everyone who loves animals and wants to learn more about this working farm in the heart of the city. There are cows, sheep and chickens, and cheese and butter are made in the dairies. The farm is open daily. Children under 14 must come with an adult.

The Local Community Sports Centre offers a variety of activities — table tennis, snooker, indoor football and karate. It is open six days a week from 5 p.m. to 10.30 p.m.; a small charge is made for the use of equipment.

The Nature Club meets at weekends, usually on a Sunday afternoon. Members take part in walks and discussions. All age groups are welcome.

The Play Centre provides free entertainment for the under fives with indoor and outdoor play areas. You may leave your child here for up to two hours at a time in any one day.

The Potter Centre is organised for retired people. It opens five days a week from 11.30 to 6.00. Cheap hot meals are provided at lunchtimes and different activities take place every afternoon. There is also a monthly theatre excursion.

The Adventure Playground in Rowan Street was built for children up to the age of 14. There are ropes, swings, slides and tree climbs with an adult in charge all the time. Open during school holidays from 9 a.m. to 5 p.m. A small charge is payable for each child.

The people below want to take part in one of these activities. Put a cross in the box to show which is the best activity for each person.

	Water Park	City Farm	Community Sports Centre	Nature Club	Play Centre	Potter Centre	Adventure Playground
1. Mr Smith has retired but dislikes being with groups of elderly people. Although he is still an energetic man he doesn't like sport; an opportunity to get away from the city would suit him.	☐	☐	☐	☐	☐	☐	☐
2. The summer term has finished and Howard wants his seven-year-old son to play somewhere safe while he is at work.	☐	☐	☐	☐	☐	☐	☐
3. Mrs Muller wants someone to look after her three-year-old daughter for an hour twice a week while she goes to typing classes. She has very little money.	☐	☐	☐	☐	☐	☐	☐
4. Steve is 16 and would like to take up a new sport. He's been thinking of trying sailing or perhaps a game he can play inside during the evening.	☐	☐	☐	☐	☐	☐	☐
5. Mark and his sister are 13 years old and full of energy. They love animals and want to be outdoors every morning but their parents are too busy to go with them.	☐	☐	☐	☐	☐	☐	☐

QUESTION 4

Read the information about the Health Club. Put a cross in the box for numbers 1–9 if a statement is correct.

Membership Types & Prices

Membership is offered on an annual basis. All prices are inclusive of tax. (Please tick relevant boxes)

Type 1 Membership
Single	£345 ☐
Husband & Wife	£475 ☐
Family*	£545 ☐
Each extra Child	£85 ☐

Type 2 Membership
Single	£230 ☐
Husband & Wife	£340 ☐
Child	£55 ☐

Type 3 Membership
Company – 6 named persons	£1,850 ☐

Guests
Adult	£3 per day ☐
Child	£1.50 per day ☐

Sun Beds
These are charged as extra on a per session basis.

Type 1 Membership is 7 days a week 7 a.m.–9 p.m.
Type 2 Membership is Mon–Fri 9 a.m.–5 p.m.
Type 3 Membership is 7 days a week 7 a.m.–9 p.m.
* Family Membership includes 2 adults and 2 children.
Children under 3 years will be admitted free of charge.

The Health & Fitness Club at the Post House Hotel, Cambridge offers a wide variety of facilities for both fitness and relaxation:

Fully equipped gymnasium – whether you are training for a particular sport, or just want to look and feel great, the gymnasium offers all you need to enjoy a variety of interesting exercise plans.

Indoor heated pool – jump in and swim or float around at your own pace. The pool is the central point for all the family, and even if you can't swim we can arrange lessons: – it's never too early or too late to learn!

Spa Bath – give yourself a luxurious break in the warm bubbles of our American style spa bath: it's a great way to relax.

Saunas – relax in our pinewood saunas, with separate rooms for men and women.

Sunbed – look healthy all year round with a fast, natural sun tan.

Expert help – professional staff can provide expert advice, design fitness plans to match your needs and offer friendly encouragement.

Open seven days a week – because the Health & Fitness Club is part of a fine hotel, it is open everyday, from early morning through to the late evening. What's more, you can enjoy the hotel's other facilities, such as its restaurants, bars and lounges, and all under one roof!

1. This health club is at a hotel. ☐

2. Only adults may use the swimming pool after 5 p.m. ☐

3. You must be a good swimmer to use the pool. ☐

4. Membership prices include all the activities and equipment. ☐

5. There is an extra charge for members' friends. ☐

6. A family with Type 1 membership that has four children will pay the same as if they had three. ☐

7. This club is suitable for serious sportsmen and women. ☐

8. Retired people can join this club. ☐

9. The staff are qualified to give advice about keeping healthy. ☐

QUESTION 5

Read this passage and then answer the questions below. You must put a cross in the correct box or write in a few words.

Parents whose children show a special interest in a particular sport have a difficult decision to make about their children's careers. Should they allow their children to train to become top sportsmen and women? For many children it means starting very young and school work, going out with friends and other interests have to take second place. It's very difficult to explain to a young child why he or she has to train for five hours a day, even at the weekend, when most of his or her friends are playing.

Another problem is of course money. In many countries money for training is available from the government for the very best young sportsmen and women. If this help cannot be given it means that it is the parents who have to find the time and the money to support their child's development – and sports clothes, transport to competitions, special equipment etc. can all be very expensive.

Many parents are understandably worried that it is dangerous to start serious training in a sport at an early age. Some doctors agree that young muscles may be damaged by training before they are properly developed. Professional trainers, however, believe that it is only by starting young that you can reach the top as a successful sports person. What is clear is that very few people do reach the top and both parents and children should be prepared for failure even after many years of training.

1. This is from ☐ a letter.

   ☐ an advertisement.

   ☐ a sports diary.

   ☐ a newspaper article.

2. What is the writer's intention? ☐ to inform us about training

   ☐ to discuss training methods

   ☐ to give details about training costs

   ☐ to suggest a training programme

3. How do some governments help young people who are good at sport?

   ....

   ....

4. Give one advantage and one disadvantage of early training.

    ....

    ....

5. Here are four extracts from schoolchildren's letters to penfriends. Put a cross in the box to show which one is the most likely to take up sport professionally.

> My two main interests are reading and playing
> tennis. I read on average two novels a week and spend
> the rest of my spare time playing tennis with my
> friends. I love sports clothes, so most Saturdays
> I spend going round the shops seeing what's new.
> Do you play any sports?

☐

> I get up every morning at 6 o'clock and jog for
> an hour before school. When I come home, I have to do
> my homework really quickly because I go down to the
> local track where I run. I train for several hours
> every evening. It's all worth it, though, when we
> have races. It's a great feeling even if you don't
> win.

☐

> The school I go to gives us a lot of homework. I usually come
> home, have something to eat, do two hours homework and
> then go to the swimming pool. I swim for three quarters of
> an hour every day. Most of my friends think I'm mad.
> Even when we go on holiday I'm not happy if I can't go
> swimming at least four times a week, so I like going
> to the coast best.

☐

> I'm very lucky, I go to a wonderful school. I enjoy it
> very much. They don't believe in homework, so I have
> plenty of time to do things that interest me. I do
> a lot of sport, I go to an exercise class, go to
> dance classes, and I swim twice a week. I love
> going to the cinema with my friends and sometimes
> we have parties. At weekends we often go on
> cycle rides into the fresh air of the country.

☐

WRITING

QUESTION 6

Here are some sentences about Tom's hobbies. Finish the second sentence so that it has the same meaning as the first.

EXAMPLE: I like swimming best of all sports.

    My *favourite sport is swimming*.

1. The teacher asked Tom whether he had any hobbies.

   'Do ....

2. 'I like tennis, swimming and football,' Tom replied.

   Tom said that...

3. He has also been collecting stamps for five years.

   He also started...

4. He has over 3000 stamps in his collection.

   There ....

5. He spends two hours a week sorting out stamps.

   Sorting out his stamps ....

QUESTION 7

You and some friends are organising a disco party. Write out the notice you are going to put up outside your school. Don't forget to include place, time, date, directions and any other information people will need to know.

QUESTION 8

Imagine you are spending a week at a Sports Holiday Camp. First, circle your choice of activities for the afternoons. Then, using this information, write a letter to your friend telling him or her how you are spending your time. Use about 80 words.

SPORTS HOLIDAY CAMP

	MON	TUE	WED	THU	FRI
A.M.	swimming	cycling	swimming	walking	swimming
P.M.	tennis OR football	horse-riding OR volley-ball	free for shopping OR activity of your choice	swimming OR football	cycling OR volley-ball

DON'T FORGET to (circle) your choice for each afternoon!

Dear . . . . ,
I am spending a week at a Sports Holiday
Camp. . . . .

....

....

....

....

....

....

....

....

....

....

LISTENING

QUESTION 9

Put a cross in the box you think is the most suitable.

EXAMPLE:

1.

2.

3.

☐   ☐

☐   ☐

4.

☐   ☐   ☐   ☐

5.

☐   ☐   ☐   ☐

6.

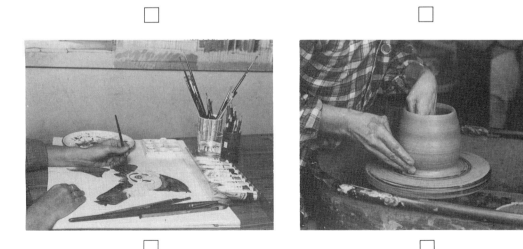

7.

QUESTION 10

Listen to this language course director describing the leisure activities for the coming week. Put a cross in the boxes you think are the most suitable.

1. In the cookery class they'll make cakes. ☐

    bread. ☐

    biscuits. ☐

    sweets. ☐

2. Tomorrow evening they'll hear poetry by students. ☐

    foreigners. ☐

    children. ☐

    teachers. ☐

3. The concert will be given by an orchestra. ☐

    a group. ☐

    a singer. ☐

    a pianist. ☐

4. The talk will be about Oxford. ☐

    a new city. ☐

    an old house. ☐

    a film. ☐

5. The Sunday walk is in the country. ☐

    some gardens. ☐

    a park. ☐

    the hills. ☐

QUESTION 11

Listen to the radio sports report and fill in the spaces in these newspaper headlines, using ONE word for each numbered space.

Two Australian motor (1)................... crash: (2)................... injuries

Lindhe wins (3)…….......... matches in a row

Hungary (4)……......... England

France and Italy to play again on (5)...................

Belgian cyclist breaks both (6)………………

QUESTION 12

If you agree with the statement, put a cross in the box under 'Yes'. If you do not agree, cross the box under 'No'.

		Yes	No
1.	United have played very well lately.	☐	☐
2.	Jones has been out of the team with a broken arm.	☐	☐
3.	In the end the two men agree that Jones is a good player.	☐	☐
4.	United sometimes kick the ball into their own goal.	☐	☐
5.	The men enjoy joking about the match.	☐	☐

Unit 4   The media

READING

QUESTION 1

Look at the five pictures of signs below. Someone asks you what each sign means. For each sign put a cross in one of the boxes – like this X – to show the correct answer.

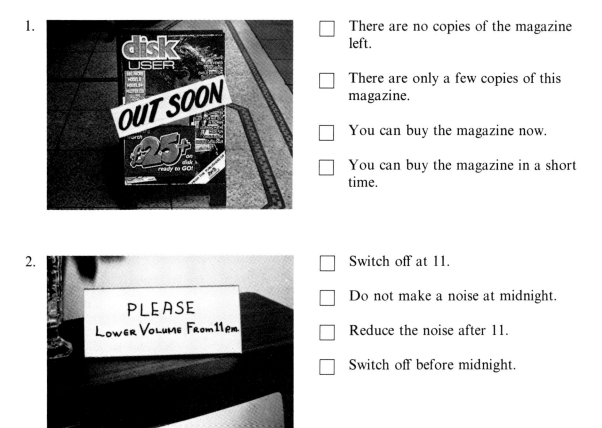

1.

☐ There are no copies of the magazine left.

☐ There are only a few copies of this magazine.

☐ You can buy the magazine now.

☐ You can buy the magazine in a short time.

2.

☐ Switch off at 11.

☐ Do not make a noise at midnight.

☐ Reduce the noise after 11.

☐ Switch off before midnight.

3.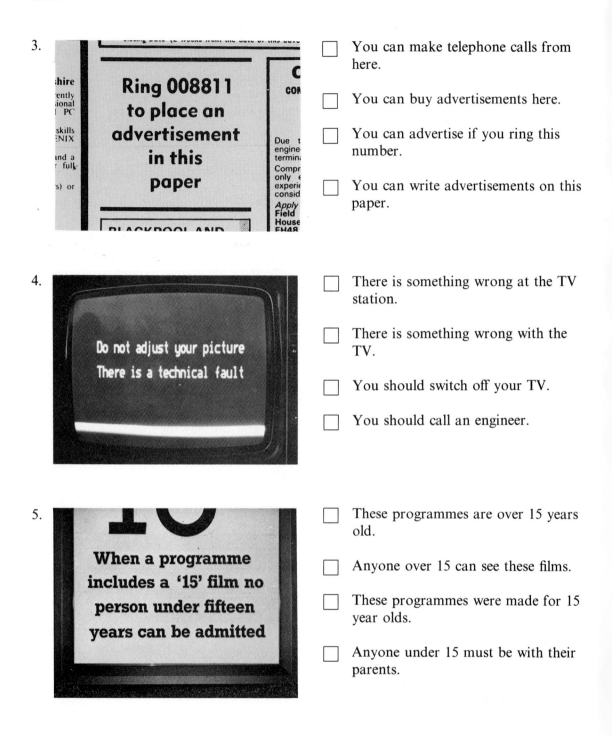

Ring 008811 to place an advertisement in this paper

☐ You can make telephone calls from here.

☐ You can buy advertisements here.

☐ You can advertise if you ring this number.

☐ You can write advertisements on this paper.

4.

Do not adjust your picture
There is a technical fault

☐ There is something wrong at the TV station.

☐ There is something wrong with the TV.

☐ You should switch off your TV.

☐ You should call an engineer.

5.

When a programme includes a '15' film no person under fifteen years can be admitted

☐ These programmes are over 15 years old.

☐ Anyone over 15 can see these films.

☐ These programmes were made for 15 year olds.

☐ Anyone under 15 must be with their parents.

QUESTION 2

Read the article below and circle the letter next to the word that best fits each space.

EXAMPLE: Did you hear the .... on the radio last night about China?

A   article   B   picture   Ⓒ   programme   D   film

There has been a revolution in the world of newspapers. Not many years (1)..............., newspapers were still being produced using techniques unchanged for (2).............. hundred years.

The journalists gave their stories to a typist, who prepared them for an editor, who passed them on (3).............. the printer. The printer, who was a (4).............. skilled man, set up the type. (5).............. was then collected to make the pages. When the pages were complete, the printing machines could be (6)...............

Nowadays what (7)...............? The journalists type their stories into a computer. The (8).............. checks their spelling, plans the page, shapes the articles. When the pages are ready, another computer may control the printing.

(9).............. can be no doubt about it, producing a newspaper is an entirely different (10)............... now.

1.   A   before   B   after   C   ago   D   yet

2.   A   a   B   some   C   an   D   over

3.   A   to   B   by   C   through   D   with

4.   A   hardly   B   mostly   C   partly   D   very

5.   A   They   B   Which   C   This   D   All

6.   A   switched   B   started   C   stopped   D   moved

7.   A   gives   ·B   occurs   C   goes   D   happens

8.   A   computer   B   editor   C   typist   D   printer

9.   A   It   B   There   C   You   D   We

10. A   skill   B   work   C   management   D   business

QUESTION 3

Below are 4 magazines on a news-stand in a railway station. Find out what each one is about and then answer the questions.

A

What's on

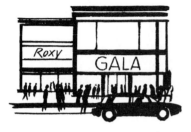

Be in the right place at the right time!

All the news and views of the sights and shows in and around the capital this week

Sightseeing by bus or on the river?

The complete theatre and film guide for all ages

B

City Guide

'A race against time' – how should we advise new businesses?

Special report on the new tax laws

Computers – do they really help your customers to understand their accounts?

C

Let's go!

Up-to-date information on the latest lightweight racing models from abroad

Speed or safety – should bike riders be asked to make a choice?

Doing your own repairs – do you really save money?

D

Follow this

All the latest styles for the very young – sew a super present!

Make the most of your money: financial advice for retired people on small incomes

"Look after yourself" – health notes for the over-sixties

⟫→

Visual material for the Oral

1A

The Garden Restaurant
MENU

STARTERS	soup	90p
	tomato salad	75p
	fruit juice	55p
MAIN COURSES	chicken	£3.50
	fish	£2.65
	today's special	£1.80

All served with a choice of fresh vegetables
or a green salad and rice or potatoes.

DESSERTS	fresh fruit	50p
	cheese	£1.10
	ice-cream (various flavours)	80p

1B

1C

2A

2B

3A

3B

APRIL

3RD MONDAY

10.30 Dentist

4TH TUESDAY

9-12 English Lessons

5TH WEDNESDAY

2.30 Cinema

6TH THURSDAY

2 pm ENGLISH EXAMS!!!

7TH FRIDAY

12.30 End of term lunch Party

8TH SATURDAY

Trip to LONDON all day

9TH SUNDAY

3C

3D

4A
BBC 2

7.25 POPEYE CLASSICS Old cartoons.

7.40 BARRY DOUGLAS. Third of five piano recitals of the work of Liszt, The Dante Sonata and his transcription of Wagner's Liebestod.

8.10 HORIZON. British class politics — have they changed?

9.00 CLARENCE. Comedy with Ronnie Barker as a removal man in the Thirties.

9.30 MOONLIGHTING. Unusual detective series, with Cybill Shepherd and Bruce Willis.

10.15 SPLIT SCREEN. Arcane double film debate about the merits and demerits of new music and electronic and computerised works.

10.45 NEWSNIGHT. Archbishop Runcie's first major TV interview this year.

11.30 WEATHERVIEW.

11.35 CRICKET: THE CENTENARY TEST

ITV

6.35 CROSSROADS

7.00 WISH YOU WERE HERE? A rail pass in Scandinavia, fly-drive in Ireland, and self-catering in Majorca.*

7.30 CORONATION STREET.*

8.00 AFTER HENRY. Prunella Scales, Joan Sanderson and Janine Wood as three generations sharing a house. The funny lines in the series on radio do not work so well on television.

8.30 WORLD IN ACTION. Education for life: interviews with school leavers from six different countries.

9.00 HARD CASES. Police drama.

10.00 NEWS AT TEN.

10.30 THAMES HEADLINES.

10.35 THE CARTIER AFFAIR. TV movie, with Joan Collins sending herself up (we hope) as a TV-soap star who falls for a thieving conman, David Hasselhoff, Telly Savalas.

12.15 I SPY.

1.15 am SPORTSWORLD EXTRA. Boxing: North American Middleweight Championship; Football: European highlights.

2.30am NEWS HEADLINES.

2.33am TAXI. High-pedigree Danny DeVito sitcom.

3.00am FILM: COME AND GET IT. (Hawks/Wyler 1936 US b/w) Epic drama from works of Edna Ferber.

5.00am ITN WORLD NEWS

Channel 4

7.00 CHANNEL 4 NEWS*.

7.50 COMMENT.

7.58 WEATHER.

8.00 BROOKSIDE.*

8.30 RUDE HEALTH. John Wells in a medical comedy that should be placed on the sick list.

9.00 MERELY MORTAL. Strange examination of death, asking doctors, a spiritualist, a philosopher, and an historian to discover if they have collected any evidence of the existence of the soul and its relationship to the body.

9.45 MASTERWORKS. Edwin Mullins discusses the picture Coastal Landscape by Victor Pasmore, at the Tate Gallery.

10.00 HILL STREET BLUES. More problems for New York police.

10.55 THE ELEVENTH HOUR ARAB CINEMA – ALYAM ALYAM. (Ahmed El Maanouni 1978 Morocco). Dramatised documentary of the hardness and shortness of Moroccan peasant life. With English subtitles.

4B

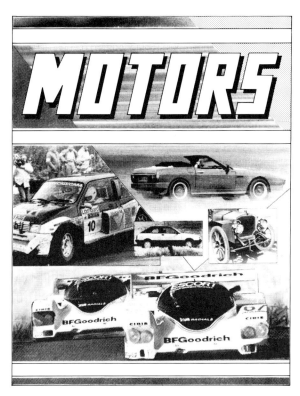

4C

5A

5B

Now look at the descriptions of these people who are waiting to catch the train to London. Write A, B, C or D in the boxes provided to show which magazine you think each of them will choose to read on the train.

1. Mrs Oliphant is travelling to work. She is a bank manager and needs to know all the news about financial affairs. ☐

2. Mrs White is an old lady going to visit her daughter. She's not rich, but she's very fond of her grandchildren and enjoys making up-to-date clothes to give them. ☐

3. Mike Johnson is 15. He's very keen on pop music and sport. Today he's going to see an international cycle race. One day he hopes he'll be one of the competitors. ☐

4. Johanna Field, a nurse, isn't working today. She has no special plans. In her free time she likes going to discos where she can dance, or to shows where she can watch top professional dancers. ☐

5. Marcus Prester is a university student. He is hoping to see some modern art exhibitions this morning and perhaps see a film in the afternoon. ☐

QUESTION 4

Look at this page from a guide to radio programmes and write the name of the programme which offers each of the following:

1. Money saving suggestions ....

2. Religious thought ....

3. International politics...

4. Cookery suggestions ....

5. Farming information ....

6. Modern music..

7. Classical music ....

8. Advice on repairs ....

6.00
Early morning news
with Mike Trant

6.15 Let us pray
Starting the day with God
Dr Sheila Jones

6.30 Market Day
News and prices for the
agricultural industry
Weather in detail
Presenter Eddie Smith
Producer Sue Grant

7.00 News
with Mike Trant

7.15
Starting with a song
Julia Burgess and Philip
Green play the latest records
by your favourite bands
Producer Philip Perkins

8.00 News
with Mike Trant

8.15
The Morning Show
Music, talk and laughter
with Fred Granger and his
guests
Producer Sonia Abdela
(Horoscopes 9.15)

10.00
What's for supper?
Today's guest Michael Wong,
with details of an exciting
way of preparing fish
Chinese style
Producer James Bowen

10.20
People and Politics
Reports and opinions from
around the country
Presenter in Edinburgh
Ian Moore, and in London
Joan Lewis
Producer Sue Grant

11.00 News
with Mary Kelly

11.10 At Home
Jim Shaftesbury and
Rowena Kirby with
information and ideas on
how to make your home
brighter, safer and cheaper
to run!
This week's special –
mending wooden furniture.
Producer James Bowen

12.00 News at Noon
The full story of today's
world news, plus interviews
and reports by Mary Kelly,
Ian Moore and Philip Green
Newsreader Mike Trant
Producer George Abrahams

1.00 Sports Ground
Results and news on national
and international
competitions
Presenter Eddie Smith

1.50 Weather

2.00 Afternoon Concert
Mozart, Haydn and other
great eighteenth century
composers
The Anglian Concert
Orchestra conducted by
Freda Felix
Recorded at Ebury
Cathedral during this year's
Ebury Festival
Presented by Julia Burgess
Producer Philip Perkins

QUESTION 5

Read this passage and then answer the questions below. You must put a cross in the correct box or write in a few words.

... and so I have watched your programme for years and have always enjoyed it. In fact it's one of the few programmes which is also suitable for children and I know that many families like ours watch it together. However, last week I was very disappointed and also very angry that no warning was given at the beginning of the programme that what was going to be shown was unsuitable for children. It is quite unnecessary to show close-up pictures of people who have been murdered. I know it's not real blood but children don't always realise this and my children were very frightened. There is also no need for people to use all sorts of bad language. Children very quickly copy what they hear and swear words and suchlike are the very things parents don't want their children to use. Newspapers and news programmes are full of all the terrible happenings in the world and I think we can expect television to provide us with an escape from reality. I don't know whether you actually enjoy unpleasant and shocking scenes but since last week I know that I for one will never watch the series again and I hope that more viewers like me will feel the same and simply switch off their sets.

1. This is from ☐ a letter.

    ☐ an advertisement.

    ☐ a magazine.

    ☐ a diary.

2. What is the writer trying to do? ☐ to inform

    ☐ to amuse

    ☐ to warn us

    ☐ to complain

3. What does the writer want television to offer?

    ....

    ....

4. Why will the writer's family never watch the programme again?

....

....

5. Which of the following shares the same opinion as the writer? Put a cross in the box under the correct one.

```
I really dislike many TV programmes in which
rich and beautiful people lead such exciting
lives.  Reality isn't like this for most of
us and so your programme which dealt with the
terrible crime of murder was a good way of
reminding us what the real world is like.
```
☐

```
Many children never watch the news on TV and so I
was very glad last week when my family and I watched
your programme on murder and what it must actually
be like to experience the effects of such a crime
when it is close to your family.
```
☐

```
Some TV producers seem unable to tell the
difference between what should and should not be
shown on family TV programmes. My family was very
upset by what they saw last week, it was as sad and
violent as the news.
```
☐

```
I know it's impossible to protect children from
hearing swear words and so it's a good idea to
include them in a programme where parents are
likely to be present. In this way we can deal
with the problem at the time, pointing out
which words one should never use.
```
☐

WRITING

QUESTION 6

Here are some sentences about newspapers. Finish the second sentence so that it has the same meaning as the first.

EXAMPLE: 'The Times' was first printed two hundred years ago.

It is *two hundred years since 'The Times' was first printed.*

1. More newspapers are sold during elections.

    People ....

2. Popular newspapers are cheaper than serious ones.

    Serious newspapers ....

3. Some newspapers have more pictures than text.

    There are ....

4. Some newspapers are more informative than others.

    Some newspapers are not ....

5. The owners of newspapers are usually very rich.

    The people ....

QUESTION 7

A group of business people in the town where you live want to start a new newspaper. They have sent everybody one of the forms below asking them to fill it in so that they can decide what sort of newspaper would be most popular. Fill in the form giving details about yourself and your opinions.

SUGGESTIONS FOR A NEW NEWSPAPER
Please answer ALL the questions

1. Do you read a daily newspaper at present?   YES/NO

2. If you answered YES to question 1 which section(s) do you most enjoy?

   ....

   ....

   If you answered NO to question 1, why don't you read one?

   ....

   ....

3. What do you think a newspaper should do?

   ....

   ....

   ....

4. What would you like to see included in a new newspaper?

   ....

   ....

   ....

5. Would you be willing to pay more for a better newspaper?   YES/NO

6. What is your occupation?

   ....

QUESTION 8

You have recently been to see the film advertised below called 'The Journey' which you enjoyed very much. Write a letter to your friend telling him or her about the film. Use about 80 words.

THE JOURNEY
- two young men and an old car
- on a thousand miles of difficult roads
- through countryside and cities

SEE THE FILM AND FIND OUT WHAT HAPPENS!

Dear. . . . . ,
How are you? I'm fine and as busy as ever but last week I found the time to go, and see a new film called 'The Journey'. It was really good. . . . .

LISTENING

QUESTION 9

Put a cross in the box you think is the most suitable.

EXAMPLE:

1.

2.

3.

☐ ☐ ☐ ☐

4.

☐ ☐

☐ ☐

5.

☐ ☐ ☐ ☐

6.

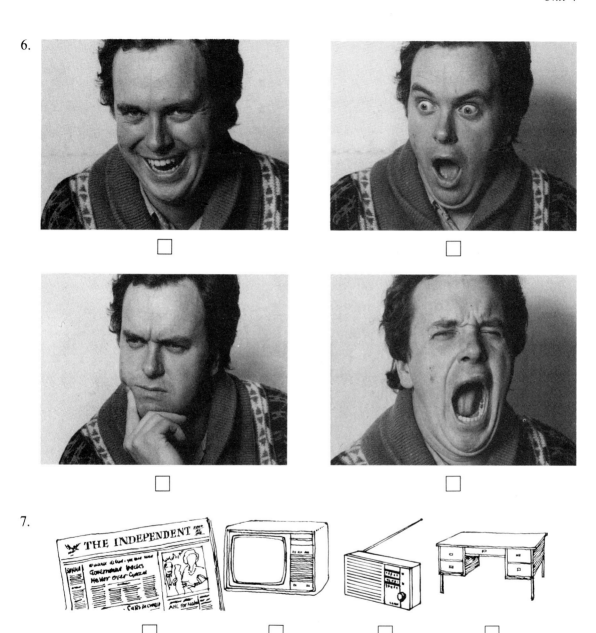

7.

QUESTION 10

Listen to the details about this evening's radio programmes and put a cross – X – in the boxes you think are the most suitable.

1. 'Lollipops' is a news programme. ☐
                  drama programme. ☐
                  discussion programme. ☐
                  musical programme. ☐

2. 'Round the World' deals with sport. ☐
                  politics. ☐
                  travel. ☐
                  economics. ☐

3. The play called 'Back to Square One' is new. ☐
                  well known. ☐
                  about the 1970s. ☐
                  about married life. ☐

4. The interview at 10.30 is with a person from China. ☐
                  India. ☐
                  Britain. ☐
                  Italy. ☐

5. The discussion programme is broadcast twice a week. ☐
                  every evening. ☐
                  once a week. ☐
                  twice a day. ☐

6. The last broadcast is news. ☐

                     weather. ☐

                     music. ☐

                     poetry. ☐

QUESTION 11

Write in the information needed below and put a cross in the boxes you think are the most suitable.

        ★ New video shop in College
(1)........................

        ★ Video films for hire at
(2)........................ price and are from
many countries, including
(3) Italy ☐ India ☐
     Austria ☐ U.S.A. ☐

        ★ Buy a radio or cassette player
and get (4)........................ audio
cassettes FREE!

        ★ Get £50 off the price of any TV
bought and paid for before 6 p.m. this
(5).....................!

        ★ For more details phone
(6)........................

QUESTION 12

If you agree with the statement, put a cross in the box under 'Yes'. If you do not agree, cross the box under 'No'.

		Yes	*No*
1.	The boy and girl disagree about 'Dallas'.	☐	☐
2.	The girl is interested in world affairs.	☐	☐
3.	The girl is impressed by the boy's arguments.	☐	☐
4.	The girl thinks the people in 'Dallas' are like real rich people.	☐	☐
5.	They agree that nobody famous reads the TV news.	☐	☐

Unit 5   PET practice test paper

READING

QUESTION 1

Look at the five pictures below. Someone asks you what each sign means. For each sign put a cross in one of the boxes – like this X – to show the correct answer.

1.

MIND
YOUR HEAD

☐ Watch out for falling bricks.

☐ Avoid this doorway.

☐ Remember to cover your head.

☐ Remember to lower your head.

2.

PLEASE

STAND CLEAR OF

THE DOORS

☐ Don't wait in front of the doors.

☐ The doors are not in use.

☐ Make a queue in front of the doors.

☐ Please use other doors.

⟫→

3.

☐ Workmen are digging.

☐ Workmen are on overtime.

☐ Workmen are up above.

☐ Workmen are inside this building.

4.

☐ Do not waste time using the stairs.

☐ Get out through the emergency door.

☐ You must use the stairs instead of the lift.

☐ Keep the road free for emergency services.

5.

☐ Leave your child here.

☐ Buy a child's present here.

☐ Please give some money.

☐ Collect your child here.

QUESTION 2

Read the article below and circle the letter next to the word that best fits each space.

EXAMPLE: The reception desk is on the ground ....

    A level   B side   C area   (D) floor

Mr Alex Fraser lived his entire life in a small town in the north of England.

He never left the house (1).............. he had been born, never married, never went on holiday and had no friends.

He worked in a local factory for (2).............. forty years but even the people who had worked with him for years (3).............. very little about him.

He wore the same old clothes year in year out, and (4).............. he shopped regularly at the local store he bought only the most basic foodstuffs, never changing his purchases from one week to the next.

So (5).............. he died last month neighbours and local people were astonished to learn that Mr Fraser was not just a rich man, he was in fact (6).................. millionaire!

He had no bank account, no money invested anywhere but in the various drawers, cupboards and boxes in his house there were hundreds and thousands of bank (7)............. and coins.

It took police over two weeks to clear the house and the bank clerks took just as long to (8).............. all the money.

'We had absolutely no idea that he had been hiding his money over the years' one of his neighbours (9)............... 'In fact we used to feel sorry for him, we thought he was a poor old man unable to (10).................. anything better for himself!'

---

1. A which   B where   C who   D what

2. A until   B above   C over   D across

3. A reminded   B held   C had   D knew

4. A although   B but   C because   D however

5. A while   B when   C during   D that

6. A the   B this   C a   D one

7. A papers   B money   C letters   D notes

8. A number   B count   C guess   D make

9. A said   B spoke   C mentioned   D told

10. A pay   B spend   C afford   D give

QUESTION 3

Below are details about different language schools in the UK. Read the details and then answer the questions.

Ensmore School, Bury, is a medium-sized school near the town centre. It is open throughout the year and offers courses at all levels. It organises week-end excursions and a sports programme during the summer months June – September. Students live with local families and have all their meals with them except weekday lunches which are provided by the school.

Queen's School, Exeter, is a beautiful old house on the edge of the city. The minimum age for entry is 16 years and all the courses require students to be resident. There are special business courses twice a year in February and October. Beginners not accepted.

Milton School, Yarmouth, is a modern school offering activity-centred courses so that each day students combine language lessons with sport and a cultural visit to a nearby place of interest. The school is in the countryside but has its own transport. All students share study bedrooms.

International School, Swansea, is a large school in the city centre which offers all students single study-bedrooms within the school. Special attention is paid to each student's progress and extra individual lessons are included in a student's programme. All levels accepted.

Grove School, Birmingham, is a modern school offering courses for people with special interests in history, music, theatre and literature. Class sizes are small – no more than 8 in each class and there is a full social programme during the week. Students live with selected families and are expected to take part in family life at weekends.

The five people below want to learn English in the UK. Put a cross in the box to show the school that is best for each person.

	Ensmore School	Queen's School	Milton School	International School	Grove School
1. Pablo is 14. He doesn't want to live with a family and he would like to do as much sport as possible.	☐	☐	☐	☐	☐
2. Julius is studying drama and would like a course which will develop this interest and allow him to spend time with English people at weekends.	☐	☐	☐	☐	☐
3. Rosa is a beginner and would like to live with a family so she can practise speaking English as often as possible, but take part in organised activities during weekends.	☐	☐	☐	☐	☐
4. Ahmed would like a school where he can have private lessons without paying anything extra, and his own room.	☐	☐	☐	☐	☐
5. Kari doesn't mind which school she goes to so long as the classes are not large and there is plenty of entertainment in the evenings.	☐	☐	☐	☐	☐

QUESTION 4

You are given this handout in the street. Look at the statements below, check the handout, and put a cross in the box if the statement is correct.

National Photographic Services Show
The Cranwell Centre, Albus St, Leeds
Monday, February 11th – Sunday, February 18th

A great range of attractions for anyone interested in photography, publicity, marketing . . .

T. Tucker & Co Ltd
"The Sharpest Blow-ups In Town"

Bring your colour slide or 35mm film and we'll produce an ENORMOUS picture from it in just the time it takes you to look round the rest of the show! Prices £10–£15 (depending on size). Special price for more than 5 prints from same original.
Stand 12

Film!! Film!! Film!!

Everything you need to take perfect photographs, whatever the lighting conditions. For every sort of camera we have every sort of film so hurry along and catch our special low prices on the first three days.

Stand 13

Alfred Reed – Outdoor clothing

Come and check our wonderful range of raincoats, umbrellas, sunhats, winterwear – all the things you need for the difficult weather conditions you meet when you go to take that special photograph.
Stand 14

M & V Photo Supplies

Equipment for the serious photographer. Also albums, films etc. 15% off on orders over £50.00 taken during the show.
Stand 15

CREEK AND WARING

Instant pictures! Instant success! Surprise your family and friends!
All our customers have fun taking photos! Enjoy a new pastime and keep your favourite memories in a handsome album – our free gift to you if you buy a camera from us before the weekend.
Stand 16

Joe Callicot – Souvenirs
Your face on your plate!

We'll take your picture and print it on a fine china plate or bowl. Or bring along your favourite black and white photograph and we'll use that. Years of experience supplying gift shops, tourist centres etc.
Stand 17

Joe Callicot – Souvenirs
Your face on your front!!

We'll take your picture (or your friend's!) and print it on a T-shirt. Choose from 3 styles in fashionable pale blue, pink or white in small, medium or large size. The ideal present. Clubs and societies – ask about our special prices for large orders.
Stand 18

Frank Bear and Sons
Specialist Booksellers

For the widest range of fine art books, photography books and magazines. Expert staff will offer advice. Rare prints and valuable rare books for the collector. Ask for our detailed list. We also have a large secondhand stock at very reasonable prices as well as up to date technical books.
Stand 19

1. The National Photographic Services Show aims to attract many different sorts of people. ☐

2. T. Tucker will take a photo of you and print it extra large. ☐

3. Alfred Reed sells photographic equipment. ☐

4. You must spend at least £50 at M & V Photo Supplies to get their cheap rate. ☐

5. The majority of Creek and Waring's customers are working photographers. ☐

6. Creek and Waring are advertising photo albums at special prices. ☐

7. Joe Callicot sells goods to shops. ☐

8. Joe Callicot prints photos on various different objects. ☐

9. Frank Bear's staff will advise you on what equipment to buy. ☐

10. Frank Bear sells old and new books. ☐

QUESTION 5

Read this passage and then answer the questions below. You must put a cross in the correct box or write in a few words.

I get a lot of letters at this time of year from people complaining that they have a cold which won't go away. There are so many different stories about how to prevent or cure a cold it's often difficult to know what to do. Although colds are rarely dangerous, except for people who are already weak, such as the elderly or young babies, they are always uncomfortable and usually most unpleasant. Of course you can buy lots of medicines which will help to make your cold less unpleasant, but you must remember that nothing can actually cure a cold or make it go away faster. Another thing is that any medicine which is strong enough to make you feel better could be dangerous if you are already taking drugs for some other illness so always check with your chemist or doctor to see whether they are all right for you. And remember they might make you sleepy – please don't try to drive if they do! Lastly, as far as avoiding colds is concerned, whatever you may be told about magic foods or drinks, the best answer is to keep strong and healthy – you'll have less chance of catching a cold, and if you do, it shouldn't be so bad!

1. This is from ☐ a doctor's notebook.

   ☐ a diary.

   ☐ a magazine.

   ☐ a school biology book.

2. What is the writer's intention? ☐ to write in an amusing way

   ☐ to give general advice

   ☐ to complain about his/her health

   ☐ to describe personal experiences

3. Who should talk to the doctor before buying medicine for a cold?

   ....

   ....

4. What is the writer's opinion of 'magic food and drink'?

   ....

   ....

5. Which of these letters is most like the letters mentioned at the beginning of the passage? Show which one you think it is by circling the letter A, B, C or D.

A I always eat lots of fresh fruit and vegetables
   and take plenty of exercise — if other people
   followed my example I'm sure we'd lose far
   fewer working days through colds.

B . . . have had it for two weeks and it's just the
   same as last year, nothing I do seems to make me
   get better.

C The best thing is to stay at home and keep warm and
   not give your cold to other people. And of course
   eat plenty of fruit.

D What really worries me is that my father, who is
   over sixty, insists on driving when he's taken
   this medicine for his cold.

WRITING

QUESTION 6

Here are some sentences about towns. Finish the second sentence so that it has the same meaning as the first.

EXAMPLE: I had never seen a more beautiful building.
It was *the most beautiful building I had ever seen.*

1. England has many old towns and villages.

    There ....

2. There are often very narrow streets.

    Their ....

3. Heavy traffic annoys the residents.

    The residents find ....

4. Sometimes a bypass has to be built.

    Sometimes the Government ....

5. That can cost a lot of money.

    That can be ....

QUESTION 7

The airline on which you were travelling home has lost your suitcase. Fill in the form below giving as much information as you can.

LOST LUGGAGE INSURANCE CLAIM FORM

FAMILY NAME ....

FIRST NAME ....

ADDRESS ....

....

....

DATE OF BIRTH ....

WHAT PIECE(S) OF LUGGAGE HAVE YOU LOST? ....

....

WHAT COLOUR IS THE LUGGAGE?...

WHICH AIRPORT DID YOUR FLIGHT LEAVE FROM?..

WAS YOUR NAME AND ADDRESS ON YOUR LUGGAGE?...

WHAT WAS IN YOUR SUITCASE? (Please give as much detail as possible, for example clothing, valuables etc.)

....

....

....

....

WHAT IS THE TOTAL VALUE OF THE MISSING CONTENTS? ....

SIGNATURE ....   DATE ....

QUESTION 8

You were one of the witnesses of a robbery in a shop and the police have asked you to make a statement in order to help them with their enquiries. Use the picture below to help you. Write about 80 words.

Policeman: Now can you tell us exactly what happened while you were in the shop?

....

....

....

....

....

....

....

....

....

LISTENING

QUESTION 9

Put a cross in the box you think is the most suitable.

EXAMPLE:

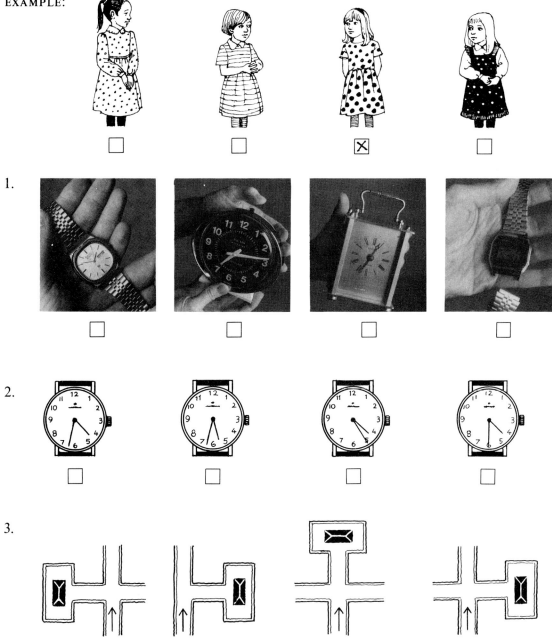

1.

2.

3.

4.

☐

☐

☐

☐

5.

☐

☐

☐

☐

6.

□

□

□

□

7.

□

□

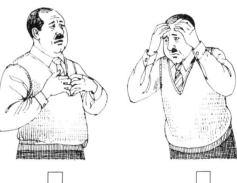

□

□

QUESTION 10

In these notes put a cross in the boxes you think are the most suitable.

1. Johnsons are looking for people to work full-time. ☐
    part-time. ☐
    two mornings a week. ☐
    three afternoons. ☐

2. Daybreak want people to work mornings. ☐
    weekends. ☐
    nights. ☐
    four days a week. ☐

3. The job at the Sports Centre offers cheap accommodation. ☐
    cheap travel. ☐
    free meals. ☐
    free uniform. ☐

4. Computers International want people willing to learn. ☐
    type. ☐
    sell. ☐
    advertise. ☐

5. The job at the Garden Centre means working in the shop. ☐
    travelling around. ☐
    working outside. ☐
    selling plants. ☐

QUESTION 11

Write in the information needed below and put a cross in the boxes you think are the most suitable.

Recommended Books

'Knife (1)....................' by Muriel Prescott
published by Greenshield Press at £7.95
action takes place in (2)....................
Mary Sutherland is a (3)....................

In a library you'll find it in the section called
(4)   travel guides ☐   short stories ☐
       gardening ☐   novels ☐

'Near and Far' by Mabel Suter
published by Victoria Press at £(5)................

In a library you'll find it in the section called
(6)   travel guides ☐   short stories ☐
       gardening ☐   novels ☐

QUESTION 12

If you agree with the statement, put a cross in the box under 'Yes'. If you do not agree, cross the box under 'No'.

		Yes	No
1.	The woman thinks the bag is ugly.	☐	☐
2.	The man suggests she hasn't looked after the bag carefully.	☐	☐
3.	The man gets very angry with the customer.	☐	☐
4.	The woman agrees to return the bag to the manufacturer.	☐	☐
5.	The man goes to find the manager.	☐	☐